My Best Book of

Ancient
Rome

Deborah Murrell

KINGFISHER

Contents

KINGFISHER

Kingfisher Publications Plc
New Penderel House
283–288 High Holborn
London WC1V 7HZ

www.kingfisherpub.com

Created for Kingfisher Publications Plc
by Picthall & Gunzi Limited

Author and editor: Deborah Murrell
Designer: Dominic Zwemmer
Consultant: Richard Platt

Illustrators: Richard Hook, Adam
Hook, Angus McBride, Simoné
Boni, Peter Dennis, Les Edwards,
Luigi Galante, David Salariya,
Ron Tiner, Thomas Trojer

First published by Kingfisher
Publications Plc 2004

10 9 8 7 6 5 4 3 2 1

1TR/0304/WKT/MAR(MAR)/128KMA

Copyright © Kingfisher
Publications Plc 2004

A CIP catalogue record for this book
is available from the British Library.

ISBN 0 7534 0958 5

Printed in China

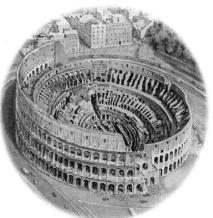

How Rome began

About 3,000 years ago, a tribe of people called the Latins settled on the hills where Rome stands today.

They had chosen a good place to live. From the top of the hills they could easily see any enemies approaching. The River Tiber below supplied fresh water, and they could reach the sea by boat. Soon, more villages grew up nearby and eventually they all joined together to form the city of Rome.

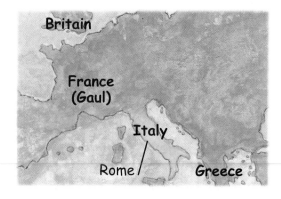

Where was early Rome?

Rome was on a fertile plain in Latium, a part of what is now Italy. To the north of Rome lived the Etruscans, and to the south lived a colony of Greek people. There were also smaller tribes of hill farmers, including the Sabines and the Samnites.

River Tiber

The hills of Rome

Rome is said to be built on seven hills. One of them, the Palatine hill, was probably the site of the first Latin villages. Later, the emperors of Rome built their grand homes there. The word 'palace' comes from the name of the Palatine hill.

The Etruscan enemy

The early Romans learned a lot from their powerful neighbours. The Greeks taught them science, architecture and the arts. The Etruscans introduced them to gladiators, chariot races and the toga. The Etruscans often attacked Rome, and by about 600BCE it was under Etruscan control. Historians believe that the last three kings of Rome were Etruscans.

Etruscan warriors attacked many Roman villages.

The Capitoline hill, below, is the centre of government in modern Rome.

Early farmers grew grains, vegetables and fruit.

Farmers used simple ploughs to prepare the land for planting.